# Good Work!
# Plant Life

Dona Herweck Rice

## Publishing Credits

Rachelle Cracchiolo, M.S.Ed., *Publisher*
Conni Medina, M.A.Ed., *Managing Editor*
Jamey Acosta, *Content Director*
Dona Herweck Rice, *Series Developer*
Robin Erickson, *Multimedia Designer*

**Image Credits:** pp.3, 12 ©iStock.com/YuriyS; pp.4, 12, Back cover ©iStock.com/fotokostic; p.10 ©iStock.com/proxyminder; all other images from Shutterstock.

**Library of Congress Cataloging-in-Publication Data**

Rice, Dona, author.
  Good work. Plant life / Dona Herweck Rice.
     pages cm
  Summary: "What does a plant need to live? It needs more than you might think!"— Provided by publisher.
  Audience: K to grade 3.
  ISBN 978-1-4938-2139-6 (pbk.)
1. Plants—Juvenile literature.
2. Plants—Development—Juvenile literature.
3. Growth (Plants)—Juvenile literature.  I. Title. II. Title: Plant life.
  QK49.R46 2016
  580—dc23
                                                                              2015013195

## Teacher Created Materials

5301 Oceanus Drive
Huntington Beach, CA 92649-1030
http://www.tcmpub.com
**ISBN 978-1-4938-2139-6**
© 2016 Teacher Created Materials, Inc.

# good soil

good water

# good food

# good light

# good space

# good air

good helpers

# Words to Know

air

light

soil

water